DAYS OF AWE

DAYS OF AWE

Stories for
Rosh Hashanah
and
Yom Kippur

adapted from
traditional sources by

Eric A. Kimmel

Illustrated by

Erika Weihs

PUFFIN BOOKS

The art was painted in oils on gessoed acid-free boards.

PUFFIN BOOKS
Published by the Penguin Group
Penguin Books USA Inc., 375 Hudson Street, New York, New York 10014, U.S.A.
Penguin Books Ltd, 27 Wrights Lane, London W8 5TZ, England
Penguin Books Australia Ltd, Ringwood, Victoria, Australia
Penguin Books Canada Ltd, 10 Alcorn Avenue, Toronto, Ontario, Canada M4V 3B2
Penguin Books (N.Z.) Ltd, 182–190 Wairau Road, Auckland 10, New Zealand

Penguin Books Ltd, Registered Offices: Harmondsworth, Middlesex, England

First published in the United States of America by Viking Penguin,
a division of Penguin Books USA Inc., 1991
Published in Puffin Books, 1993

3   5   7   9   10   8   6   4   2

Text copyright © Eric A. Kimmel, 1991
Illustrations copyright © Erika Weihs, 1991
All rights reserved

LIBRARY OF CONGRESS CATALOGING-IN-PUBLICATION DATA
Kimmel, Eric A.
Days of awe: stories for Rosh Hashanah and Yom Kippur / adapted
from traditional sources by Eric A. Kimmel; illustrated by Erika
Weihs.
p.   cm.
Previously published: New York, N.Y.: Viking, 1991.
Summary: Three tales present the ideals of repentance, prayer, and
charity that are the basis of Rosh Hashanah and Yom Kippur.
ISBN 0-14-050271-8
1. High Holidays—Legends.   2. Legends, Jewish.   [1. High
Holidays—Legends.   2. Folklore, Jewish.]   I. Weihs, Erika, ill.
II. Title.
[BM693.H5K56   1993]   296.4'31—dc20   93-583   CIP   AC
Printed in the United States of America   Set in Cloister

For Vera Petersen

—E.A.K.

Contents

Days of Awe

Rosh Hashanah, Yom Kippur, and the ten days between them mark a period of the Jewish calendar known as the High Holidays. In Hebrew, they are called *Yamim Noraim*—"The Days of Awe." The High Holidays are celebrated in early autumn, usually between the beginning of September and the first two weeks in October. The exact date changes from year to year because the Jewish calendar is based on the moon's cycles and has 354 days per year—this varies from the solar calendar commonly used in the West.

"Rosh Hashanah" means "Beginning of the Year." It is a joyous festival. Apple slices are dipped in honey as a symbol of hopes for a year filled with sweetness. The traditional hallah loaves are sometimes baked in the shape of ladders, expressing the wish that good fortune may ascend for all during the coming year.

Yom Kippur, "The Day of Atonement," is also a time for new beginnings. It is a solemn, though not somber, day. On Yom Kippur, we are called upon to reflect on our deeds of the past year. Have we made the most of our opportunities? Have we fulfilled all our promises and obligations? Have we done something to be ashamed of? Now is the time to repay, to repair, to ask forgiveness.

No period in the Jewish year is as moving as the Days of Awe. On the two days of Rosh Hashanah and the day of Yom Kippur, the entire congregation gathers in the synagogue for services that begin at sundown, continue in the early morning, and end a little after sundown the next day. It is a time out of time as the centuries-old ritual unfolds. People wander in and out; small children run up and down the aisles. The congregation rises, sits down, then rises again. The cantor's voice soars. The Torah scrolls are brought out and paraded around; people press forward to touch them. The urgent notes of the *shofar*, the ram's horn, punctuate the drone of murmured prayers.

On Yom Kippur, all this is intensified by a twenty-four-hour fast. Lack of water and food makes the hours pass slowly. By late afternoon, some of the older people no longer have the strength to stand. The smaller children have been taken home. But as sundown approaches, the intensity builds. People return to take their places for the *Ne'ilah* service. In their minds, they see the gates of heaven slowly closing as the sun sets. Physically and emotionally drained, they rise to add their voices to the final prayers. At last the sun goes down. One drawn-out note of the ram's horn brings the day to a close. The members

of the congregation leave the synagogue to return to the world of everyday concerns. "*Shanah tovah*," they say to each other, "*G'mar hatimah tovah*"—"May you have a good year. May a good year be signed and sealed for you."

Jewish tradition teaches that, in the course of these ten days, God examines the lives of all human beings. He considers their actions and their nonactions; their good deeds as well as their not-so-good deeds. Then He determines their fate for the coming year. In the words of a familiar prayer, "On Rosh Hashanah, it is written, and on Yom Kippur, it is sealed."

Zusya of Hanipol, a nineteenth-century Hasidic rabbi, once commented, "When I am called to give a final account before the Heavenly Throne, I am not afraid of being asked, 'Why were you not like Abraham?' for then I will answer, 'Because I am not Abraham.' And if I am asked why was I not like Moses, I can answer, 'Because I am not Moses.' But if I am asked, 'Why were you not like Zusya?' what will I say then?"

During Rosh Hashanah, and especially on Yom Kippur, we are called to give an account of what we have done with our lives. The themes of repentance, prayer, and charity are repeated over and over again. Repentance forces us to confront the difference between ourselves as we are, and as we might be. Prayer brings us before the Infinitely Vast Power Who creates and sustains whole worlds, and by Whose Will we live or die.

Finally there is charity, by which we remember our fellow human beings. Charity, the rabbis say, is most important of all, for without compassion for others, there can be neither true repentance nor meaningful prayer.

Tshuvah—Repentance.

Tefilah—Prayer.

Tzedakah—Charity.

These are the gates to the Days of Awe.

The Samovar

A Story about Charity

Jewish tradition is uncompromising on the subject of charity. If a hundred beggars come to your door and only one is truly needy, you must give to all of them for the sake of that one.

An amusing story is told about Rabbi Zusya of Hanipol. Though well loved, he was extremely poor. He wandered from town to town, trusting in the charity of his followers. One man made it a point to help him generously. The man's affairs prospered. Soon he became very rich. Then he thought, "If giving to a pauper like Zusya brings me such luck, imagine how much better off I would be if I gave money to a really important rabbi!" So he stopped giving to Zusya and instead sent off large donations to all the great rabbis of the land. Immediately his luck took a turn for the worse. His business failed. Within a month, he had lost everything. Rabbi Zusya did not forget him. He made a special trip to comfort him.

"I don't understand it," the man told Zusya. "I did so well when I gave to you. But when I gave to the great rabbis, everything crumbled."

"The explanation is simple," said Zusya. "When you gave charity with a free hand, without really thinking about whom you were giving to, God did the same. But when you began looking around for a truly worthy recipient, so did He."

We give charity not so much for others as for ourselves. It is part of a circle. Charity teaches compassion. Compassion leads us to charity.

It was the eve of Rosh Hashanah. Rivka, the glovemaker's wife, was preparing for the holiday that began at sundown. She shaped lumps of dough into two round loaves of hallah and set them in the oven next to the iron pot that held the stew. As she shut the oven door, she brushed back a strand of gray hair that had escaped from under her kerchief.

"I am glad no guests are coming for this holiday," she said to herself. "A handful of small potatoes with a scrap of meat hardly deserves to be called a stew. The hallah is little better. Just the scrapings of the flour barrel. But what can we do? At least Haskel and I have something to eat. There are plenty of people who do not even have that."

It was true. Times were bad. People flocked to the cities looking for work, but there was no work to be found. "This was a bad year," Rivka thought. "But maybe the next one will be better. I will pray for that."

She had just poured herself a glass of tea when she heard a knock at the door. "Another beggar," she groaned, as she rose to answer it. Beggars had been coming by all morning. Rivka felt ashamed that she had so little to give them, especially today, on the eve of Rosh Hashanah, when people should do all they can to help those less fortunate. The knocking came a second time. "I'm coming, I'm coming," Rivka said. She reached into her apron to see if she had a coin to give. Then she opened the door.

"Good day! Are you the lady of the house? May I come in?"

In the doorway stood an officer dressed in a spotless white tunic with enormous epaulets on his shoulders. His splendid mustache gleamed as brightly as his polished black boots. He carried a large bundle wrapped in oilcloth.

"Yes, of course. . . . Come in, Your Honor," Rivka stammered, not at all sure she should invite a stranger into her house but uncertain how to refuse. "May I offer you some tea?"

The officer set his bundle on the kitchen table. "Tea? No, I haven't time. I imagine you're wondering what this is about. I've been posted to a distant province and I am unable to take my samovar with me."

"Samovar?"

"Yes, to make tea. It's right here." He tapped the bundle

with his carefully manicured forefinger. "It's a family heirloom. Very old. Very precious. I cannot leave it with just anyone. You and your husband were recommended highly. Would you be so kind as to take care of my samovar while I am away?"

"Certainly," Rivka heard herself saying. "It doesn't take up much room. Perhaps we could keep it for a little while."

"Excellent! You won't regret it. That samovar always brings good luck." He started toward the door.

"Sir . . . !" Rivka called after him. The officer turned.

"Yes?"

"When are you coming back?"

"Don't expect me for at least seven years," he replied with no more concern than if he were going down the street to the tavern.

"Seven years!"

He disappeared out the door before Rivka could finish the sentence.

"Wait! Come back! I'm not sure I want to keep your samovar. Not for seven years!" She hurried to the doorway, but by the time she reached it, he was gone. Rivka looked up and down the street. "Where did that officer go?" she called to a group of boys playing with a top in the alley.

"What officer?"

"The one who just left my house. He was wearing boots and a white tunic."

The boys stared at each other. One of them gave Rivka a peculiar look.

"Oh, you're no help!" She went back into the house and shut the door. "Well," she said, turning to the bundle, "if you're to be our guest for seven years, I'd better have a look at you." She untied the string and unwrapped the oilcloth. As the officer said, it was a samovar. But, for a supposedly precious heirloom, it was in terrible condition, black with tarnish and covered with cobwebs.

"This looks like something that fell off a junk wagon!" Rivka exclaimed. "Well, if it's going to stay in my house, it has to be clean." She rinsed out a rag and wiped off the dust and cobwebs, but when she tried to polish the samovar, she failed completely. Nothing worked, not even the special polish she used for her grandmother's Sabbath candlesticks. The samovar remained as black as soot.

"I've tried my best. This will have to do." Rivka set the samovar on a shelf while she checked the oven to see if the hallah loaves were done. Just then she heard another knock at the door. "Oh, no! Not another officer!" To her relief, it was only a beggar.

She gave the man a coin, apologizing that she could not give more. He thanked her. When she went back into the house, something about the samovar caught her eye. It was still black, but now she could definitely see a thin streak of polished

· 19 ·

brass shining through the tarnish on its base. Rivka took the samovar down from the shelf to examine it more closely. No, that streak had certainly not been there the last time she looked. Could the tarnish be so thick it took the polish several minutes to work? Rivka had never heard of that before, but that did not mean it could not happen. Once again, she sat down with polish and rag.

Nothing happened. She rubbed and rubbed, but the shining streak did not get wider. Yet it was *definitely* there. And Rivka was equally certain that it had not been there when she opened the door for the beggar.

The hallah was ready. She took the loaves from the oven and set them by the window to cool. An old woman passed by in the street. "Mrs. Gutman! Mrs. Gutman!" Rivka called. "Wait! Don't go so fast. We had extra flour, so I baked a hallah for you. Here it is."

The old woman clutched the warm bread in her thin arms. "A blessing on you. May you live a long life," she murmured through pinched lips. Mrs. Gutman was a widow who lived in the attic of the house at the end of the street. Her husband, a candlemaker, had died the year before. She was barely able to pay her rent.

Rivka added more water to the stew, then closed the oven door. "Should I have given her that hallah? The one that's left is so small. But how could Haskel and I eat two loaves,

knowing that poor Mrs. Gutman does not even have one? That tiny loaf may be all she will have this evening. Better for her to take it. It would stick in my throat." She glanced over her shoulder at the samovar. A polished patch of brass no bigger than a thumbnail gleamed on the handle. Rivka gasped. "That wasn't there before! What witchcraft is this?" She took a towel and threw it over the samovar, determined to have nothing to do with it until her husband came home.

She expected him at three, but it was half past four when he finally appeared, puffing and sweating, having run all the way from his shop. Haskel the glovemaker was not a man given to running anywhere. Rivka knew at once that something had happened.

"You won't believe this! I don't believe it myself!" Haskel blurted out before his wife had a chance to say anything. He threw himself down in the nearest chair and wiped his face with his handkerchief. "I had just closed the shop when a carriage stopped in the street outside. A nobleman got out. He had on white gloves, a frock coat, a tall beaver hat, and carried a gold-headed cane. He walked over to the shop, stuck a monocle in his eye, and began looking at something in the window. I couldn't imagine what he found to interest him. There was nothing on display except one pair of gloves. Then he saw me standing inside. He rapped on the glass with his cane and motioned to me to open the door. It was already a quarter past three and I wanted to get home to get ready for the holiday. I tried to tell him the shop was closed, but he paid no attention. I heard his voice through the glass: 'Open up. You won't be sorry. I want to talk to you.'

"What could I do? I unlocked the door and let him in. He pointed to the gloves in the window.

"'Those gloves. I want to buy them. How much?'

"I couldn't believe my ears. You know which gloves he was talking about? The ones I made for that coachman who died before they were ready. His widow didn't see why her husband needed a pair of new gloves to be buried in, so she refused to pay. I put them in the window, hoping someone might want them. But I never expected a nobleman to be interested.

"'They're ordinary leather gloves,' I told him.

"'Nonsense,' he scoffed. 'I know quality work when I see it. How much do you want for them?'

"I shrugged. 'Five crowns?'

"'Is that all? Don't be silly. These gloves are easily worth a hundred and that's what I'll pay.' He opened his wallet and threw down a fistful of hundred-crown notes. I nearly fainted. There were over two thousand crowns there! 'I want you to make nine more pairs for me,' he continued. 'Here is the money in advance.' Then he went to the window, picked up the gloves, got in his carriage and drove away. Can you believe it,

Rivka? Two thousand crowns for ten ordinary pairs of gloves!"

"Today, Haskel, I can believe anything." Rivka removed the towel and took the samovar down from the shelf. Then she told her husband the story of the officer's visit.

"Strange things are happening. I don't know what to make of it. Could it be the work of evil spirits? Maybe we should ask the rabbi?"

Haskel agreed. They left the samovar standing on the table and hurried to the rabbi's house. The rabbi's wife did not like to see her husband disturbed on the eve of such an important holiday, but when she saw how frightened the glovemaker and his wife were, she let them in.

They followed her to the study where the rabbi sat poring over a thick book. He looked up as the couple came into the room.

"What is wrong? Did someone die?"

"No, Rabbi," Rivka began. "No one died. I'm afraid it's worse, much worse. Today my husband and I were visited by evil spirits." She started telling her story. When she finished, Haskel told his. "Rabbi, what do you think?" they both asked at once.

"Hmmm." The rabbi stroked his beard. "You ask me what I think? I don't think you were visited by evil spirits. Evil spirits bring bad luck, not good fortune. In my opinion, Rivka, your visitor was the Prophet Elijah himself. Good fortune will come your way as long as you have that samovar. But as he told you, at the end of seven years, he will come to claim it. Then everything will be the way it was before."

"But what should we do?" Rivka asked.

"I cannot tell you that," the rabbi said. "I do know this. You have been given seven years of good luck. Use them well."

Rivka and Haskel walked back to their house more bewildered than before. Seven years of good luck. The rabbi was right. They should use them well. But how?

All at once, Rivka had an idea. "Haskel! The samovar! I polished it until my arms were sore and nothing happened. But after I gave a coin to a beggar and a hallah to poor Mrs. Gutman, it grew brighter." She grasped her husband's shoulders. "Don't you understand what that means?" Haskel blinked. "Never mind. Trust me. The money the nobleman gave you, where is it?"

"Here, in my pocket."

"Quick, give it to me!"

"What are you going to do with it?"

"You'll see."

Rivka hurried to the marketplace where the last remaining vendors were already closing up their stalls. She stopped at the fishmonger's.

"Do you still have that beautiful fish I saw this morning?"

"Unfortunately yes," the fishmonger told her. "Times are bad. No one can afford to buy it."

"I can," Rivka said, throwing down a hundred-crown note. "Deliver it to Widow Gutman. You know where she lives."

Rivka went around to all the other stalls buying the last of the bread, meat, vegetables, and pastries, and ordering it delivered to poor people all over town. She bought everything in the market.

"Rivka! You're throwing away money like dirt!" her husband wailed.

Rivka paid no attention as she hurried back home, Haskel following, grumbling that good fortune had disturbed her wits. But it was Haskel who gasped in amazement when he saw the samovar on the kitchen table. Nearly all the tarnish was gone. Rivka was not surprised.

"It *was* the Prophet Elijah! Now I know why he came. We have been granted good fortune so we can help others. Listen, Haskel. Promise me that no matter how much money comes our way, we will use only what little we require for ourselves and give the rest to others."

None of this made sense to Haskel, but Rivka was so sure she was right that she soon persuaded him. For the ten days from Rosh Hashanah until Yom Kippur, no beggar who came to their door went away without receiving alms and a big parcel

of meat and bread. Rivka and Haskel gave away money without counting.

By the time the holidays ended, all the money was gone. Haskel returned to his shop with a heavy heart. But, to his astonishment, when he arrived there, he found the whole street filled with noblemen and noblewomen standing in line outside his door waiting to place their orders for gloves. Haskel sold gloves as fast as he could make them. He bought more materials, hired more workers, rented a whole building for his workroom. Prosperity had no end. But he and Rivka remained true to their promise. Out of all the wealth that came their way, they took no more than their simple needs required. The rest they used to help others.

Seven years passed.

On Rosh Hashanah eve, as Rivka was readying the house for the holiday, she heard a knock at the door. She opened it. There stood the officer. Rivka recognized him at once, for though seven years had passed, he looked exactly as she remembered him.

"I was expecting you," she said. "Your samovar is ready." She pointed to a bundle wrapped in oilcloth standing on the kitchen table.

"I see," the officer said. "I'll take it off your hands now and trouble you no further."

"Oh, it was no trouble at all. And just as you said, it did

bring us luck. I even polished it for you. I hope you don't mind. You might wish to inspect it, to be sure it isn't damaged."

"Very well," the officer said. "I'll have a look at it, if you like." He untied the string and folded back the oilcloth. The gleaming brass lit up the room like a chandelier filled with candles. There was not a trace of tarnish anywhere.

The officer turned to Rivka. For the first time, she noticed how soft his eyes were, how filled with kindness and wisdom. "Do you know how old this samovar is?" he asked.

"I have no idea."

"It is older than the world. And in all the years of its existence, no one has taken better care of it than you. I believe you have earned the right to keep it."

"Keep it? Oh, no, I couldn't. It doesn't belong to me. Besides, it's really too big for the shelf." Rivka glanced at the samovar. When she looked up, the officer was gone.

Rivka and her husband Haskel lived to an extremely old age. Their prosperity increased every year. But from all their wealth, they took only enough for their own simple needs. The rest they used to help others.

The samovar remained on the shelf in the kitchen. Those who saw it say it gleamed brighter than a thousand suns.

The Shepherd
A Story about Prayer

What is prayer? It is opening our hearts to God, expressing our overwhelming joy in being His creatures and thanking Him for giving us life.

The Mahzor, the High Holiday prayer book, contains many beautiful prayers, some centuries old. But prayers that come from the lips and not the heart are only mumbled words. It is not necessary to pray in Hebrew, or even in a synagogue. A simple song chanted in a field can be equal to the prayers of the most learned rabbi. And infinitely more precious.

A shepherd once pastured his sheep in a field outside the city of Córdoba. He did not know how to read or write, nor could he say any prayers; no one had ever taught him. But that did not stop him from praying. The shepherd so loved God that he simply made up his own prayers out of whatever thoughts came to mind. This is how he prayed:

"God, if You had sheep, I would take care of them as if they were my own. And I would charge You only half what I charge everybody else for looking after them. And if You didn't have any money, I would take care of them for free. That's how much I love You."

And at other times he would pray:

"God, if You were hungry and I had radishes, I would give You half my radishes. And if You were still hungry, I would give You all of them. That's how much I love You."

He would go on like that, day or night, shouting out prayers as his heart moved him.

One day a famous scholar passed by the field on his way to attend the High Holiday service at the Córdoba synagogue and chanced to overhear the shepherd saying his prayers.

"God, if it was raining and You didn't have a hat, I'd lend You mine. And if my hat wasn't big enough to keep You dry, I'd lend You my cloak. And if that wasn't enough, I'd stand over You and let the rain fall on me. That's how much I love You."

"What nonsense is this!" the scholar scolded the shepherd. "Do you think that He Who made the heavens and the earth needs you to keep the rain off Him?"

The embarrassed shepherd did not know how to reply. "Forgive me, Rabbi. I meant no harm. I was only saying my prayers."

"You call that idiotic twaddle 'prayer'? What an igno-
ramus! Has no one ever taught you to pray properly?"

The shepherd shook his head.

"Come over to the fence. I will teach you."

The shepherd left his sheep and came over to where the
scholar stood. The learned man then delivered a long lecture
about the different prayers, their origin and meaning, and the
prescribed order of the service. "From now on, either pray
properly or don't pray at all," he warned the shepherd. Then
he continued on his way to the city.

The shepherd now faced a terrible dilemma. He had not
understood a word of the scholar's lecture. Nor could he
remember any of the prayers the scholar tried to teach him.
Yet he was ashamed to go back to his own way of praying
because he thought it was wrong. The shepherd did not know
what to do, so, bewildered, he stopped praying entirely.

God's Throne stands on the highest pinnacle of heaven. Yet if
a single downy feather falls from the breast of the smallest
bird, He is aware of it. He hears spiders spinning their webs in
dark corners. He listens to bees buzzing among summer
flowers and hears the gnat's whine at evening. The sounds of
the world form a vast symphony whose every note God hears.
Thus He knew one day that something was missing. The

shepherd who pastured his sheep outside the city of Córdoba had ceased to pray.

God summoned an angel. "My beloved servant, the shepherd of Córdoba, no longer says his beautiful prayers. He has lost his way. Go down and help him."

The angel went down and found the shepherd in the field, sitting sadly among his sheep. "Shepherd," the angel said to him, "The Holy One no longer hears your voice. Why do you no longer pray?"

The shepherd lowered his eyes. "My prayers are no good."

"Who told you that?"

"A learned rabbi. He called them 'idiotic twaddle.'"

"He is wrong. He does not know. He has never heard the Hosts of Heaven."

"How do they pray?" the shepherd asked.

"Like you," the angel said.

"Oh, I should like to hear that."

"Then you shall."

Enfolded in the angel's wings, the shepherd rose into the air. High above the clouds he flew, past the moon and stars, until he came before the Eternal Throne where choirs of angels—Ophanim, Seraphim, Cherubim—poured out choruses of prayer like waves of silver light.

"If You had sheep . . . " sang the Cherubim.

"If You were hungry . . . " the Ophanim replied.

And the Seraphim answered, " . . . I'd stand over You and let the rain fall on me."

The shepherd listened, astonished. "The Hosts of Heaven pray just like me!" he exclaimed.

"That is because, like you, they pray with a pure heart. That is the way you should pray. Always."

The angel carried the shepherd back to his pasture. Once more the shepherd lifted his voice in joyous prayer:

"God, if You were hungry and I had radishes, I would give You all of them."

And the Hosts of Heaven answered, "That's how much I love you."

Rabbi Eleazar and the Beggar
A Story about Repentance

No human being is perfect. We all make mistakes, and when we do it is important to set right the wrongs we have done; asking forgiveness from those we have injured is part of the process. Forgiving is difficult sometimes, especially in the case of people we dislike or those who have hurt our feelings. Refusing to forgive can be a way of getting even. The rabbis realized this. Looking at a world filled with endless hatred and violence, they understood how important it is to know how to bend; to be able to forgive when we actually may not feel very forgiving. That is why they taught, "Always be gentle as the reed, never unyielding as the cedar." Forgiveness is not only for the sake of those who ask it of us. It is also for our own sake.

In the beginning of the month of Tishri, Rabbi Eleazar ben Shimon journeyed from the Academy at Yavneh to his home in Migdal Gedor to spend the holidays with his family. Along the way he passed through the village of Tekoa. The people of

Tekoa were honored to have such a famous scholar in their midst. They conducted Rabbi Eleazar to the synagogue and begged him for a *"davar Torah."* He obliged with a sermon. He spoke of the potter at his wheel, the weaver at her loom, the blacksmith at his anvil. He told the inhabitants of Tekoa, "Just as these artisans shape the raw material according to their needs and inclinations, so too does the One Who Made Us All mold each of us to His purpose."

Now among those who came to hear the sermon was a deformed beggar who lived in a ruined tower outside the village. Ashamed to enter the synagogue because of his appearance, he stood listening outside the door. Rabbi Eleazar's words touched his heart. The beggar hurried home and waited beside the road. When the rabbi rode by on his donkey, he approached and asked a blessing. Startled by the man's appearance, Rabbi Eleazar gasped without thinking, "Heaven shield me from such ugliness!"

"Ugly, am I?" the man replied. "Then go to the One Who Made Me and say to Him, 'How ugly is this vessel You have formed!'"

Rabbi Eleazar blushed with shame. Not only had he humiliated an unfortunate, but he had violated his own teaching to cherish all creation. He turned to the beggar with lowered eyes. "I have wronged you. I spoke without thinking. I am deeply sorry. Forgive me."

But the beggar's humiliation rankled. "I will forgive you when the One Who Made Me forgives you," he said.

Rabbi Eleazar got down from his donkey. He took off his sandals, tore his robe, threw himself down on the ground, and heaped handfuls of dust on his head. "Forgive me. I cannot go from this place until you do."

"Come or go as you like. It is all the same to me," the beggar replied. "But as for forgiveness, as I said, I will forgive you when the One Who Made Me forgives you."

So Rabbi Eleazar remained lying in the dust at the feet of the beggar, who ignored him.

In Migdal Gedor, the hour of evening prayer was rapidly approaching with still no sign of Rabbi Eleazar. Fearing the worst, his four sons and his daughter set out to look for him. They found their father lying in the road a mile from Tekoa; clothes torn, head covered with dust, sprawled at the feet of a hideous beggar.

"Father!" they cried, rushing toward him.

"Whom are you addressing thus?" the beggar asked them.

"Are you blind? Do you not recognize our father, our teacher, the great Rabbi Eleazar?"

The beggar replied, "Are you his children? Do you

follow his example? Do you mock the poor when they ask your blessing?"

"Do not speak lies. Our father would do no such thing," said Rabbi Eleazar's oldest son.

Rabbi Eleazar raised his head from the dust. "The man does not lie. It is true, every word. I am guilty. I beg his forgiveness."

Rabbi Eleazar's second son turned to the beggar. "Why will you not forgive him?"

The beggar replied, "He has not offended me. He has offended the One Who Made Me. When He forgives him, I will."

Rabbi Eleazar's third son spoke next. "What more do you require? Our father admits his error. He humbles himself before you. You must forgive him."

The beggar turned his back. "I will forgive him when the One Who Made Me forgives him."

Rabbi Eleazar's fourth son scowled at the beggar. "Scoundrel! Be warned. If you think your life is miserable now, it will seem like paradise compared to what will come if you do not forgive our father this instant."

The beggar stubbornly repeated what he had already said before: "I will forgive him when the One Who Made Me forgives him."

Then Rabbi Eleazar's daughter came forward. She spoke

to the beggar gently. "My friend, the One Who Made You has already forgiven our father. He is always ready to forgive. His mercy, like the rain from heaven, falls on all who seek it. Our father requires nothing from you. Instead, he afflicts himself for your sake. He understands the bitterness of withholding forgiveness, of storing up malice like stones. He will not leave this spot until you accept his apology and drop this bitter burden from your shoulders. Come, say with me the words 'I forgive.' Begin the new year with a clean heart."

The beggar, whose life since birth had been one endless round of abuse and misery, felt himself moved in a way he had never known before. Rabbi Eleazar's daughter offered him her hand. He took it. They approached Rabbi Eleazar together. The beggar bent low to lift the sage from the dust. "I forgive you, Rabbi," he murmured. "Can you ever forgive me?"

Rabbi Eleazar answered, "It is already done." Then he arose and called for a new robe which he placed not on his own, but upon the beggar's shoulders. He and his children lifted the man onto his donkey and together, with song and rejoicing, they continued to Migdal Gedor.

Notes to the Stories

"The Samovar"

This is one of the oldest and best known stories in Jewish folklore outside the Bible. Its first written versions appear in the *Midrash Ruth Zuta* (1100–1200) and the *Yalkut Shimoni* (1200–1300). The classic version is I. L. Peretz's short story "Seven Years." I have added the samovar as a concrete symbol of the couple's seven years of good luck and the good deeds that entitle them to keep it.

"The Shepherd"

I found the original version of this story in Volume III (Folktales) of Micha Joseph bin Gorion's encyclopedic collection of Jewish legends, *Mimekor Yisrael*. Bin Gorion cites the *Sefer Hassidim (Mekitse Nirdamim)*, edited by Y. H. Wistynezki in Berlin in 1891, as his source, though the tale is undoubtedly much older. I have given it a Spanish setting and made one major change. In the original the scholar is visited in a dream by supernatural beings that threaten him with dire consequences unless the shepherd resumes praying the way he did before. I preferred to let the angels do it.

"Rabbi Eleazar and the Beggar"

The original version of this story appears in the Talmud in *Tractate Taanit*. The famous academy at Yavneh was founded in the first century C.E. Migdal Gedor's exact location is unknown. Tekoa, a mountain village on the border of Judea, was the home of the biblical prophet Amos.

A Personal Note

I am a storyteller, not a folklorist. What's the difference? A folklorist is a scholar who strives to be extremely precise about a story's sources. A folklorist collects stories as they are told and does not tamper with them. A storyteller, on the other hand, is an artist, one link in a long chain of tellers that goes back before the beginnings of recorded history. A storyteller sees stories as living things, constantly growing and changing. Storytellers always add something of themselves to the stories they tell. That is their art.

A long tradition of storytelling runs in my family. My grandparents, Morris and Clara Kerker, were noted tellers. They came from the Kolomea district in the foothills of the Carpathian mountains. This is a vitally important area in the history of Jewish folklore for it was in these mountains that Israel ben Eliezer, the Baal Shem Tov, achieved the insights and visions that led to the founding of Hasidism. The Baal Shem Tov was the greatest Jewish storyteller who ever lived. I like to imagine my Kerker ancestors among the group listening in a country inn or village square as he told his stories. If nothing else, they walked the same forest paths and breathed the same mountain air. I hope a portion of that inspiration has come down to me.